I0465650

The author is one of the most renowned judges of the Federal Courts based in the United Arab Emirates. He ranked in the judiciary hierarchy till he presided the Federal Supreme Court, thus being the first Emirati citizen to hold such high judicial position. The author is a holder of a Ph.D. in Public Law, as well as two high Diplomas in Political and International Relations Sciences. What really distinguishes our author is the fact that he has combined both practical and theoretical aspects; where in addition to his work as a judge, he has also been an instructor at the Judicial Institute and has participated in the discussion of many university theses. Further, the author has written many books and papers in the legal and judicial field.

On the merits of the author:

"Judge Abdulwahhab Abdool is one of the most prominent and esteemed Emirati public figures in the legal and judicial field."

— The General Secretariat of the Union Cabinet

"He is the justice and the law advocate."

— Al Bayan Newspaper:

"Your Excellency, Counselor, Dr. Abdulwahhab Abdool, you will always remain a strong beacon in the United Arab Emirates and a torch that will light the way for future generations."

– Muhammad Abdul Rahman Al-Jarrah, the judge of the Federal Supreme Court about Dr. Abdulwahhab Abdool, upon reaching his age of retirement.

For everyone,
Who wants justice, and strives for it.

Abdulwahhab Abdool

ON JUSTICE

AUSTIN MACAULEY PUBLISHERS™

LONDON * CAMBRIDGE * NEW YORK * SHARJAH

ISBN 9789948831501 – (Paperback)
ISBN 9789948831518– (E-Book)

Application Number: MC-10-01-5518616
Age Classification: E

First Published 2021
AUSTIN MACAULEY PUBLISHERS FZE
Sharjah Publishing City
P.O Box [519201]
Sharjah, UAE
www.austinmacauley.ae
+971 655 95 202

Table of Contents

Opening Verse

In the Name of Allah, the most Gracious, the most
Merciful
"So follow not the lusts (of your hearts), lest you avoid
justice"
Surat An-Nisa (135)

Warning

Words on Justice

❖ *The day of justice for those, who are unjust is more severe and disturbing than the day of injustice for those, who are oppressed.*

Ali bin Abi Talib

❖ *It is fair for a man to bring excuses to his opponents as much as he brings for oneself.*

Ibn Rushd, the philosopher

❖ *The nearest reference of justice is putting oneself in the other man's shoes.*

Jamal Al-Din Al-Afghani

❖ *Justice on earth will make the jinn cry should they hear of the same and shall make the dead laugh should they were resurrected.*

Gibran Khalil Gibran

❖ *The worst kind of injustice is pretended justice.*

Plato

❖ *There is no equality among humans, this is what justice meant for!*

Friedrich Nietzsche

❖ *For me to be harmed as a result of admitting the truth, is better than the truth to be harmed by my reluctance to admit the same.*

Victor Hugo

❖ *It is unjust to ask others what you are not ready to do!*

Quote

In the Name of Allah, the most Gracious, the most Merciful

Foreword

Since I reached the age of retirement, upon the presidential decree that was issued for the same, it has crossed my mind to write some words on "Justice." I felt it in myself to write in such field and to delve into it, due to my judicial experience in both judicial and legal justice that exceeds thirty-eight years I had spent in the investigation and adjudicating sector. This experience qualifies me to say few words about justice; especially that the speech in every gathering, every meeting and every little talk usually turns to the subject of justice and the constant complaint that it is either missing or emptied of its moral and legal content.

In these words, I address justice as an absolute value and as a relative human value, without referring to references and literature, because I only want to say some words about justice.

With these words, I do not intend to write a reference book about justice, as such may takes a long time and needs to study dozens, even hundreds of books and references on the subject. But I think a few papers are more than enough, in which I present my analysis of the content of justice philosophically and legally, hoping reach a deeper understanding of the reality of justice.

May Allah guide our steps...

The author

Introduction

Is justice real or mere illusion? And if it is real, what is its true nature? Is it an absolute value or a relative human value? If justice is an absolute value, then where is its place?... Is it in the heaven realm or among human realm? And what are its characteristics?... If justice is a human value among human beings, what are the sources of its existence? And why did it fail to maintain its purity, clarity, and absolute? What is justice as a human value? Is not the justice, which we promote for in most of the cases, a compulsive and obligatory justice – in most cases – and unequal consensual justice in part?

This book answers all these questions, inquiries and interrogations in an easy and a simple way through a philosophical and legal analysis of the content of justice, whereby the writer concludes that justice in its reality is only a tool of oppression owned by the state, like the army, security, parties, and the media, only it is a soft tool of execution through the so-called organs of justice.

May Allah guide our steps...

The author

Knowledge of Justice and the Difficulty of Defining It

"Knowledge of justice" focuses on addressing justice as a value. It is meant to examine the reality of justice, its sources, types, methods, approaches, and institutions in addition to its definition. The term "knowledge of justice" refers to this huge intellectual product produced and created by man through writings, sayings, symbols, shapes, and movements about justice, which constitute the basis of what has become known as "knowledge of justice." This knowledge is inter-disciplined with other sciences such as philosophy, ethics, sociology, law, politics, and other human sciences until it has become convenient to say that "knowledge of justice" means "the science of justice." Despite the large number of solid scientific and non-scientific studies that tackled "knowledge of justice," the definition of "justice" has remained intractable!

The reason why it remained intractable, is because its value nature makes it difficult to define.

Philosophers, ethicists, and legal scholars have agreed that justice is a human value and due to such fact, the awareness of justice, its essence and core, by man, is achieved through his knowledge and understanding of the law or rules of the movement of life and through the state of his society in terms of the degree of social, economic, political, cultural, and religious development and progress. Man varies in the proportion, amount, and degree of such awareness from one person to another, which results in a relative understanding of justice and hence relative justice. For example, if ten people of different social statuses, ages, educational qualifications, and cultures were asked to provide a definition of justice, each of them would have a different definition from the others. Accordingly, the content and theme of such definition will vary based on the social, economic, political, and religious circumstances of his saying, which leads to the multiplicity of definitions of justice. Such multiplicity of the definition of justice as well as of its content, is what makes justice more difficult to define.

What makes justice more difficult to define is the ambiguity of the "idea of justice." The idea of justice (i.e. the mental perception of what is just) is not unified or fixed in the human community. This perception varies according to the elements of time and place. In the ancient civilizations bordering the Mediterranean, such as the Egyptian, Greek, and Roman civilizations, the idea of justice meant "righteousness"...integrity in speech and uprightness in action. Accordingly, legislations were developed. As for the civilization of Mesopotamia and especially for the Babylonians, the idea of justice meant (protecting the higher ranks of society). In the major monotheistic religions (Judaism, Christianity, and Islam) the idea of justice meant (conscience). The conscience is the hidden voice rooted in the human soul, which guides the individual to distinguish right from wrong and what is good and what is horrid. In modern philosophies, the idea of justice is based on the degree or amount of "pleasure and pain."

The geographical and natural environment of human groups plays a role in the difficulty of giving a definition of justice.

In desert societies where sources of livelihood and water are limited, the idea of justice is based on the common ownership of such sources. Perhaps this idea is the same as what was mentioned in the Prophet's (May Peace Be Upon Him) hadith, "People are partners in three: pasture, water, and fire." In aquatic societies, where rivers and agriculture exist, the idea of justice is based on "sufficient water distributing." In marine societies, where the sea is the source of livelihood, the idea of justice is based on leaving the sea open. This idea is the basis of the fairness of the principle of "open sea" which is known in international law.

In brief, "justice" is still difficult to define.

The Essence of Justice

Justice is a demand for every human being and a requirement in every word or action made by him. Rather, it is a requirement for the integrity of his life. Still, human thought did not agree to give a clear and specific concept of the essence of justice, in the event that the essence of a thing is different from the type of thing, different from the nature of such thing, different from the effect of the thing and different from the definition of the thing.

The essence of justice is a field that was addressed by philosophers, legal scholars, religious scholars, and sociologists. Everyone sees justice from their jurisprudence, knowledge, and specialization point of view. Thus, any attempt to identify the essence of justice is conditional to the understanding, jurisprudence, and knowledge of those, who seek to define it. Some of those seekers do master the knowledge behind such concept, others are well established in it, while others have so little knowledge of the same.

Due to such discrepancy, any statement that is alleged about the essence of justice is only as much as the knowledge and understanding of the one, who states it.

When a law researcher analyzes "justice", what can he say about it? Is justice a human need? Or is it a human requirement? Is justice a material thing or a moral one? Is it one of the human values, or one of the absolute human values that belongs to the metaphysical world?

I find myself among those, who argue that justice, from the human perspective, is a "human value," in the sense that human life is not upright in a way that preserves his humanity and preserves his dignity, except with the duty to establish justice.

The duty to establish justice is rooted in the human conscience, divine commands, the opinions of philosophers and thinkers, and the reasons for human civility. The human conscience is that hidden call deeply rooted in the human soul, which commands its owner to be fair verbally and non-verbally. According to such understanding, conscience is based on a sound instinct that Allah has placed in man ever since he breathed the soul into his body. The degree to which a person obeys the call of conscience is affected by the surrounding circumstances, the environment in which he lives and the values and ideals upon which he was brought up and believed in.

As for divinity, God is either one God in the heaven, unique in essence and in the perfection of attributes and names...extending his dominion and power over the entire universe, or several gods of different essence, attributes, and places. The commands descending from God require due obedience and compliance. Among the divine commands, the necessity of establishing justice. The value of divine commands lies in the fact that they are a compulsory and obligatory religion for those, who believe in the same. Moreover, they believe that following and acting upon them brings them goodness and God's approval.

The opinions of philosophers and thinkers come as a third source for the necessity of establishing justice as a human value. "Justice" has occupied the minds of philosophers and thinkers since ancient times, so they dealt with it with contemplation and thinking and elaborated on its explanation and clarification of its meaning. They also enumerated its forms and pictures and indicated its place among human values. They designated its impact on the progress and civilized societies. In Greek philosophies, Plato and his virtuous republic was present and in Islam there were al-Farabi and his virtuous city as well as Ibn-e-Sina and the idea of a just city.

Furthermore, Justice ranked in a prominent place occupied by philosophers of the Enlightenment such as John Locke, Jean-Jacques Rousseau, Montesquieu, Descartes, and others.

Within the core of the views of philosophers and thinkers emerged ideas that now represent basic rules in litigation procedures in all judicial systems in the world. Such as the rule providing "no person shall be punished for one act twice," the rule "the appellant shall not be harmed by his appeal" and the rule "false does not entail a right" in addition to others.

Among their opinions and ideas calling for the necessity of administering justice, the judicial sayings that have risen to the ranks of the unwritten legal rule, such as "slow justice is injustice," "justice is the foundation of kingship" and others were woven.

As for the motives for human civilization, the facts of history indicates that the civilizations known to mankind and the progress made by man in the fields of applied sciences, social sciences, and various human knowledge, would not have occurred in this way, had it not been for the rule of justice. Without justice, it is not possible to give any grouping, human action, or intellectual progress the name of "human civilization," because justice is what gives human action its civilized and moral dimension. Justice is the environment or the gracious incubator and it – justice – is necessary for any human civilization. Such necessity is what made human experience underline the golden rule that adorns the issuance of most constitutions of Arab and Islamic countries that "justice is the foundation of kingship."

As long as justice is an element of the integrity of human life, well-being and happiness, then justice becomes a basic need that man must obtain, should he not obtain justice, he will feel pain, as is said of "need" in economics.

Despite the fact that justice is a basic and necessary need, its significance for man is borderline. Meaning that a man needs justice and there is no doubt regarding such, still he does not need it except to the extent that his needs are satisfied. Here, we can give an example of this with table salt. Salt is one of the essential and basic needs of man and food may not be acceptable without it, but in the end, man's need for salt is limited, because his need for this substance has a certain limit and so is justice. Justice is a critical need. A person does not need it more than his needs. It is not hoarded to trade upon the ascending of its value.

And it can be stored to benefit from it when it is lost and it is not credited in the accounts as capital.

Despite the marginality of justice, the need for it is permanent, recurring, and renewed. It is *permanent,* because justice is not a seasonal commodity that a person needs in certain months and seasons of the year. Rather, it is a permanent need that a person needs as long as such person is alive. He needs justice from the day he is born and even before he is born until the day he dies.

Justice is a *recurring* need i.e. a person needs it repeatedly throughout his life, he needs it for his criminal security, social security, economic security, and in all areas of his daily life.

Justice is also a *renewed* need, as it is a human value that is renewed according to time and place. Hence, what is seen within a specific historical moment context, or in a particular place (society) as justice, may not entail the same in another historical moment or in another place (society). Justice renews itself!

Measurements of Justice

When man was unable to provide a solid comprehensive definition of justice, he began to search for a criterion by which he can measure justice. So, his mind came up with a criterion for what is called "pleasure and pain." This standard finds its basis in a philosophical doctrine attributed to the Greek philosopher Epicurus. It was also adopted by some European philosophers in the modern era, such as Jeremy Bentham, John Stuart Mill, and John Locke.

The idea of this doctrine – upon its development – is based on the fact that pleasure is good and virtue and pain is evil and vice and that pleasure does not exist except through the exclusion of pain and that a person must live a virtuous life in order to feel pleasure, because the preponderance of the balance pleasure means that human life becomes a source of more pleasure.

The application of the "pleasure and pain" scale to measure justice raises controversy such as how two contradictions "pleasure and pain" can be used for justice to be measured! In other words, by applying such, we argue justice is sometimes pleasure and pain at other times while knowing that pleasure is good and a virtue and pain is evil and a vice!

Philosophers deny the existence of any contradiction in the doctrine of "pleasure and pain" when applied to justice as a human value. Pleasure is the amount of joy or extroversion or pleasure that the soul reaches. It is either material or moral and it may be temporary or permanent. As for pain, it is what afflicts the soul from distress, fatigue, or sadness. The pain may be physical or moral, such as the pain that befalls a person from losing his money, position, reputation, or freedom. In the balance of joy and distress, extroversion and distress, pleasure and sadness...etc., justice is achieved. We will see more clarification of such when explaining the types of justice.

The measure of "pleasure and pain" is clearly reflected in the legal rule. This rule is designed to control the behavior of people, who are not self-identified by various conflicting facts and in which the interests of those addressed by the rule intersect. Among the functions of such rule, restoring balance to these interests if they are violated in contravention of the requirements of the rule.

Restoring the balance is by implementing the "pleasure and pain" scale. Whoever violates the legal rule and causes harm or corruption will be faced with the penalty decided in such regard, whatever the type, amount, softness, or harshness of such penalty. This breach brings benefit to one, who is addressed by the legal rule and pain to another addressee with the same rule. Whoever is affected by pain will be rewarded with "pleasure" and whoever is affected by pleasure or delight in the breach will be rewarded with "pain." This is the "equivalence of justice," because it is a reciprocal justice for one act, which is a violation of the legal rule.

The following example illustrates the equation. The victim of a crime (for example) suffers from it and the perpetrator receives a personal benefit from the same, regardless of the type, form, and nature of this benefit. If he believes that he took his revenge on his enemy, removed an opponent from his path, or that he inflicted punishment on a rival...etc.

The measure of "pleasure and pain" achieves "equivalence of justice." The victim in the previous example is rewarded with "pleasure" and the perpetrator is rewarded with "pain." The pleasure of the victim is to enable him to redress his pain, either through retribution, compensation, penal punishment, or by any other method.

The activation of one or more of the compulsion mechanisms is 'pleasure.' The pain of the perpetrator of the crime is prejudice to his freedom, his financial responsibility, or his reputation...etc.

Since the measure of "pleasure and pain" in the previous example is codified with legal rules, the measured justice is legal justice. Just as the "pleasure and pain" scale is suitable for measuring legal justice, it is also suitable for measuring the rest of the types of justice, as will be explained later.

Justice in its Absolute Value or Justice in Heaven Realm

Absolute in philosophical thought, meaning, complete or fixed, free from every restriction, exception or condition, or pure from every designation or limitation. It is characterized by stability and universality i.e. it is not related to a specific place, a specific group or to specific circumstances or conditions. All values that are associated with the concept of absoluteness become an absolute value. Absolute values maintain their eternal characteristics, features and characteristics, they do not change or alter. Justice remains as justice; mercy remains as mercy and beauty remains as beauty as long as such values are safe away from hands of man.

But the question is where are the absolute values? Where is it located? Is it on earth? Or somewhere else other than Earth?

In all ancient civilizations and in all major monotheistic and non-celestial religions, the idea prevails that there is a connection or communication between the upper world (heaven) and the earthly world (Earth) and the underground world (the lower world). In fact, some ancient religions such as Zoroastrianism, Mesopotamia, the religions of the Egyptian civilization, and other eastern religions, decide that there is a relationship between heaven and earth and they hold that the god or gods who created the heavens and the earth inhabit the upper world "the world of heaven" and that they I descended to Earth and created the Earth and the Underworld.

The monotheistic religions, especially the major ones, also dealt with this relationship. The Jewish religion tells about the story of the creation of man and the formation of the earth and the descent of man on it and about the relationship of heaven to earth through the messengers and prophets, especially the story of the Ten Commandments that Allah revealed to the Prophet of the Children of Israel, "Moses." The Christian religion confirms such relationship more and says that God (Lord-Father) incarnated in human form and descended to earth in the name of "Jesus" or "Christ" to redeem people from their sins and save them from the same. This relationship is evident among Muslims in the revelation "Gabriel," as well as in the incident of Al-Isra and Al-Miraj and the revelation of the verses of the Qur'an. All these civilizations and religions hold that the beings and creatures of the upper world are more honorable and purer than the creatures and beings of the earthly world and that the latter is better and more honorable than the creatures and beings of the lower world.

Thus, civilizations and religions believe that there are relations between the earth and the sky and relations between the earths "the earthly world" and the underground "underworld" where the jinn, demons and spirits and that in the ability of man, who is one of the creatures of the earth, to subjugate the creatures of the underworld to his will. There are references in the books of the heavenly religions that the Prophet of the Children of Israel, King Solomon bin David, used to harness devils and jinn to accomplish heavy and hard work. There are still those, who believe in this kind of relationship between the earthly and the lower worlds.

When analyzing the upper world, jargon over the naming of such world is crowded out. Some of them say "the world above" and some of them say "the world of the unseen" and some of them say "the world beyond nature," that is, beyond the visible, the seen and the sensible. These are all designations of this world i.e. the upper world.

Personally, I prefer to use the term "Realm of the Pleroma." It is a term mentioned in the Holy Quran and according to the interpreters of the Holy Qur'an, this term means "the angels," but I see that the interpretation of Pleroma as angels, is an interpretation of the texts of the Qur'anic verses that mentioned the word "The Pleroma." But the term "the Pleroma" in the world of the Unknown, the Supernatural World, exceeds in its meaning more than angels, it includes all creatures and existents in the world of the Unknown, the Supernatural World, the world of heaven, "the upper world." The planets, stars, water, air, fire, lightning, light, brightness, and spirits. All of these things are existents within the scope of the concept of the Pleroma.

One of the beings of the heaven realm is the "Absolutes." Absolutes are spiritual values that philosophers, moral, and logic scientists have used to describe the actions of human beings, as if we say: voluntary actions and involuntary actions, voluntary actions and managed actions, beneficial actions and harmful actions, actions that inherit responsibility and actions that deny responsibility and beautiful actions and ugly actions, just actions, unjust actions, etc.

Philosophers called these absolutes the term "absolute values." Among the absolute values is "justice." Justice as an absolute value finds its basis in the laws of creation "the rules of creation." Those are the laws enacted by Allah so that his creatures, the human, may live, cherished and honored. Such as the laws of motion and stillness, the laws of the alternation of night and day, the laws of hearing and sight, the laws of good and evil, the laws of ugliness and beauty, the laws of justice and charity...etc.

And as long as the justice in the Pleroma represents an absolute value, it is permanent and never vanishes and it is infinite and unlimited and it is for everyone without limitation, pure without contamination and absolute from every condition or exception.

But justice does not remain in its absolute value when it is among the realm of man, because he is then subject to the applicable laws of the Earth.

Justice Among the Chiefs (Mla'a)

The Chiefs (Mla'a), in language, they are the masters of the people, their nobles, the prestigious once, and the upper class. It bears the meaning of power groups and lobbies in a state and in the decision-making institutions thereof. Perhaps this meaning is clear in the Qur'anic verse (20) of Surat Al-Qasas: [And there came a man running, from the farthest end of the city. He said: O Mūsā (Moses)! Verily, the chiefs are taking counsel together about you, to kill you...].

Chiefs can only be found on earth, since it implies basically the mankind, who is an inhabitant of the earth. However, the word "Chiefs" can be interpreted in a broader sense, that is, in the sense of all the creatures living on earth, including animals, birds, insects, reptiles, plants, and others. Qur'an referred to such meaning in verse (38) of Surat An-Naml, when Solomon asked those around him from the chiefs, who are among the jinn, men, birds, and other creatures, can bring him the throne of Bilqis from her kingdom of Sheba.

It is known from philosophy by necessity, that any absolute who descends from the highest (the upper world) to a world of man (the earthly world) shall lose its essential qualities and characteristics that keep him absolute due to the power and authority of the laws of the earth (the earthly world), including just as an absolute value. In the Qur'an there are references to such fact, that the creatures and beings of the realm of the Pleroma, if they descend into a realm of man (the earthly world), it shall be affected by the laws of such world. Verse (96) of Surat Al-Isra says: "Say: If there were on the earth, angels walking about in peace and security, we would certainly have sent down for them from the heaven an angel as a Messenger." The significance of this verse is that the laws of heaven are different from those of the earth. If God had sent to mankind an angel as a messenger, they would not be able to confront him, nor learn from the same, nor to see him. These references appear more clearly in the verses that talk about the story of Adam while he was in the heaven realm, where he lived in a world free of trouble, hardship, and pain, still he disobeyed Allah, so Allah sent him down to the earth "the earthly world" where Adam was subject to the laws and rules of this world.

He suffered hunger, thirst, and pain and realized his need for clothing to cover his private parts and other needs.

When justice becomes earthly, it is inevitably subject to the laws and rules of the earth that change its absolute qualities and characteristics. Among the laws and rules of the earth, time and place, power and strength, ideology and ideas.

Justice, Time and Place

By this subtitle I do not mean to discuss time and place in their philosophical and scientific dimensions. Or the discussions about them among philosophers, or what scientists discovered from the physical theories in this regard. All I mean by this heading that justice is affected by the time and place imposed by the laws and regulations of the Earth. What may be considered just in a certain period of time, is unjust in a later time. The collective penal responsibility was just in the ancient laws and it is not so in our current laws. Debtor enslavement was an aspect of the fulfillment of debt in medieval laws and it is not the same in the laws of civilized nations. The justice of the marine environments is also different from the justice of the desert environments. It also differs from the justice of mountain environments, due to the different laws and regulations of these environments.

Justice in the Earth (the earthly world) is at the mercy of time and place. It can only obey them in their changing facts and events... Why should it obey them? Because it lost its absolute value, it became the justice of time instead of time of Justice.

Justice, Power and Authority

Power is a system of domination exercised by one group over another, it takes many forms, including violence sometimes and law and judiciary at other times. The power is the fruit of strength. Wherever there is power, it generates authority and this power in the political sphere means order and submission that leads to the creation of unequal relations between the ruler and the ruled.

Authority (meaning control and domination) is one of the laws of the land that accompanied man in all stages of his intellectual and societal development, starting from the authority of the father all the way to the authority of the state in all its forms and political systems. The authority affected justice by coloring it in its own color.

When the power is oligarchic monopolized by a small group of society that enjoys the power of money, lineage, or military power and controls the political decision, then justice becomes an oligarchic justice that speaks to the interests of this group.

When the authority is an aristocracy controlled by a social class that sees itself as the best class and the elite group, that is, it is the class that is excellent in morals, intellect and knowledge, then justice is also an aristocracy that takes into account the interests of this class.

The same is the case when power devolves to a group or party that believes in the totalitarian system, in which the individual has no role or place, except through his relationship with authority.

When the authority imposes itself as the envoy of divine mercy. Justice will be a tool for confirming and consolidating the concept of the divine delegation of authority.

If this is the justice of the authority.... what is left for justice of authority!!!

Justice, Ideology and Ideas

Ideology is the set of values, ideas, and beliefs a person believes in that influences his or her worldview. Or it – ideology – is the set of values, ideas, and beliefs that a group adopts, which affects its thought and makes it see things according to its own logic, not by the logic of things in their reality. The person who looks at things from an ideological view, means that he evaluates things and weighs them with his own standards and interprets the facts in a certain way that makes them conform to what he believes to be true.

Justice in its origin and truth is an absolute value, but as soon as a person adopts it and believes in it through his ideas and values that he believes in, then justice turns into ideological justice, that is, covered with the nature of those ideas. If the ideology that the group believes in or the person in power believes in is religious, then justice is religious and if that ideology is capitalist, then justice is capitalist, but if it is socialism, then justice is socialist and so on...

The ideologization of justice takes place by modifying the concept of absolute justice, by defining its concept, mechanisms and work tools and ways and means of reaching it, in accordance with the philosophy and ideology of the group. Wherever capitalism is the state's ideology, justice becomes active in protecting individual property and freedom in all its forms and kinds and raising the status of the individual regardless of his level in the social ladder. Constitutions and laws are drafted in this direction and courts work to enshrine these values and so in the rest of the ideologies, the justice of the ideology replaces the ideology of justice.

Justice... In All Its Forms

When justice becomes in the realm of man and under the influence of the laws and regulations of this public, this justice is varied in its types and descriptions. Sometimes it is absolute justice, sometimes relative justice, sometimes divine justice, sometimes human justice, sometimes legal justice and sometimes judicial justice and when analyzing the content of each justice, its problem arises, which prevents it from being real justice. Which is evident by analyzing the content of each justice.

Absolute Justice

"Absolute justice" is described as natural justice and man has no say in making it, bring it about or control it, because it is subject to eternal laws and regulations that are beyond the nature of human laws. It is equal justice for all people. Everyone is equal in death and life, in need for food and drink and in aging. Every human being receives sunlight as much as he needs without distinction between male or female, young or old, sick or healthy, religious or not, honorable or lowly. Every person enjoys the alternation of night and day, the change of seasons of the year, the succession of the days of the week, the weeks of the month and the months of the year. Every person suffers if he has a disease or gets harmed, or loses a loved one or an expensive possession...etc. Everyone enjoys this justice and suffers according to what they need and as much as they deserve.

This view of absolute justice is true, but it is problematic. The sun and the air, health and disease, youth age and old age, the succession of days, weeks, months of the year and other facts, are in fact elements of absolute justice and they are components that enter into the construction of "absolute justice." These elements and components are self-contained events that have their own laws and have functions that go beyond the limits of man and his needs.

The basic principle is that man takes his needs of these elements to the extent he needs and in this he is like all other creatures that share the characteristics of life with man, reproduction and death, such as animals and plants that live on planet Earth. But, what differentiates man from other creatures is that his enjoyment of the aforementioned elements is not always available to him. Intentional human obstacles may prevent him from enjoying its benefits. These obstacles are the sway of power and strength. The monopolist of power and authority, with the means and tools of coercion and force he possesses, can control the amount of elements of absolute justice that the individual under his authority needs, depriving him of them or overburdening him with them, thus disrupting the measure of "justice" and in turn, the amount of pain and pleasure.

When the authority places its opponents in basements and deprives them of benefiting from the light and heat of the sun and of enjoying the succession of days, weeks and months, or it liquidates members of a religious, ethnic or political sect, or deliberately causes their death, by these actions it has deprived them of benefiting from the principle of "people's equality in benefiting from the elements of absolute justice." Since the absolute does not accept the exception, the violation of the right of one beneficiary leads to the loss of justice in the characteristic of absolute.

Therefore, the authority of human beings over each other turns the idea of "absolute justice" into a myth. Because the realm of man with its own laws, norms, and regulations, does not accommodate any absolute whatever, so how is the case with "absolute justice."

Relative Justice

Relative justice is understood as the difference between one person and another in the amount of "pleasure and pain" that he obtains as a result of the intervention of human in it. This type of justice often appears in the distribution of rights and duties or the enjoyment of services.

The humans' will that influences relative justice is either a "sinful" will or a "regulating" will. The will is "sinful" when it intervenes to prevent a group, sect, or human group from obtaining its adequate needs from rights, or to increase the number of duties placed upon it to the point of exhaustion and suffering. As it eases the shoulders of another sect or group from these duties and increases the number of rights granted to them.

When members of the ruling party obtain all the benefits and services of state agencies and institutions, while others obtain a part of them, which do not even meet their basic and necessary needs and requirements, then distributive justice becomes relative justice resulting from a sinful human will.

As for the "regulating" will, although it practically leads to disparities in people's access to rights and obligations, this inequality is based on a public interest. When the state imposes a judicial fee on hearing cases before the courts, whoever pays the fee will consider his case and whoever is unable to pay it is deprived of hearing, which creates relative justice in obtaining the right to sue. But, this relativity is based on the idea of "public interest," which here is regulating the right of litigation and not leaving it plundered by every reckless plaintiff, gloated person, or archenemy. The same applies to other rights and duties.

The problem with this type of justice is that it is based on human will. This will determine its degree, amount, scope, beneficiaries, time, and place. Not any humans' will is qualified to administer this justice, but it is the will of the one who possesses power and authority and whoever relies on them controls this justice.

By distributing this justice, the authority does not seek the good of its beneficiaries, as much as it aims to consolidate and assure itself that its orders and decisions are just. It is not an example that it was confirmed by the means of soft power or the hard power that it monopolizes.

Even when the will of the authority is a "Regulating" will, that is, the will to organize and distribute rights and duties, it intends by that to confirm itself that it is the owner of the command and the prohibition in distributing this type of justice.

In conclusion, power is the basis of justice.

Divine Justice

Divine justice is presented as the judgment that God commands. Whether it is a heavenly deity worshiped or an earthly deity sanctified. Such justice comes in the form of texts "rules" written and codified in sacred books attributed to God, revealed to a prophet, messenger, or mediator. The followers of every belief (religion) see that the commands of their God are true justice. There is no injustice or unfairness in it. Although its appearance may suggest inequality, yet in its essence and core, it is justice that the human mind cannot comprehend. It is justice that is not measured or estimated by the worldly "pain and pleasure" standards and criteria, but is estimated to the extent that the individual achieves in terms of pleasure in the God he worships and this faith pleasure is the essence of divine justice.

This presentation of "divine justice," which suggests its identification with "absolute justice," conceals within it the fact that this "divine" justice is no different from other types of justice in the realm of man. In its foundation, existence and manifestations, it is under the control of the forces of the deep state represented by the clerical class of various classes, grades, names and divine, theological and religious ranks.

The clergy, its sheikhs and jurists monopolize the function of interpreting the sacred texts, clarifying their dimensions and goals, the reason for their rulings and the punishment for those, who violate them. They are the ones who decide (by their human nature), what is divine justice and what is non-divine justice. This is the problem of divine justice.

Human Justice

Human justice is the voluntary distribution of benefits and interests among human beings. The scope of this justice is the distribution of benefits in a reciprocal manner, with one party providing a benefit and a beneficiary party giving in return for it. The seller provides the commodity and the buyer pays for it and the state provides a public service and the beneficiary of it pays its fee or wage.

Human justice appears in the form of contracts and agreements, with many names and different centers of their parties (sale contract, lease contract, insurance contract...etc.) (seller/buyer, lessor/tenant, insured/insured...etc).

This justice appears to be reciprocal and equal, but by analyzing its content and dismantling its structure, it becomes clear that it is captive to the influence of factors that make it unable to perform its social and legal function.

Among the factors that influence it, is the human will. This will, with all its awareness and moral freedom, is what shapes this type of justice and gives it its form, subject, scope and extent, with all the impulses of good and evil, selfishness and scarcity, sacrifice and selfishness, mercy and cruelty.. etc. Justice comes colored by these tendencies.

Among the active and influential elements in this justice are power and authority. Whoever owns them sets the rules by which the distribution takes place and even controls the methods, amount and time of distribution. Even when the distribution is reciprocal, contracts and agreements are often unequal between the two parties, as in contracts of submission, administrative contracts and reconciliation contracts between creditor and debtor...etc. The concept of authority and power expands to include authority, economic power, legislative power, and religious authority and power.

Timing comes as an influential element in human justice. The existence of this justice is linked to three unstable elements, which are will, place, and time. The humans' will is subjected to, afflicted, or tainted by defects, changes or transformations, which makes it unqualified, valid or capable of distributing benefits and interests. The change and alteration of the human being's location necessitates the change and alteration of the benefits and interests that he obtains, whether in terms of their type or amount. The benefits and interests of those, who reside on barren land are not the benefits and interests of those, who reside in an industrial city full with movement and life. The human need of the twenty-first century for benefits and interests is different from the need of his ancestors from previous centuries.

Judicial Justice

"Judicial justice" is defined as, the amount of "pleasure and pain" achieved by a ruling, decision or order issued by an authority authorized to issue such a ruling, decision or order. The sentence issued for imprisonment of the offender brings pleasure to the victim, his relatives and everyone, who have been harmed by the offense committed by the offender. To the same extent, the sentence brings pain to the offender who will lose his freedom for a period of time, as he spends his time behind the prison walls. The judgment issued for the termination of a contract, brings benefit to the contracting party requesting the termination because it will return it to the state it was in before the conclusion of the contract. While the same provision brings equal pain to the other contracting party, who will be deprived of the benefit that he was hoping for from the conclusion of the contract. Therefore, wherever the judgment, decision, or order achieves an equilibrium between "pleasure and pain," there is "judicial justice." This justice has its problem, which will be clarified when speaking about "Instruments of Justice."

Legal Justice

Legal justice is the pleasure and pain that are prescribed and pre-determined by legal rules. This kind of justice comes from the law. What is meant by law in this context is the law in its broad general sense, which includes written sources (legislation) and non-codified sources such as custom, general legal principles, rules of justice and equity, rules of natural law and others.

Since the law is the source of justice, "legal justice" identifies with the legal base to the degree of unity and integration in the role and function performed by the legal base, such as achieving individual security, political and economic goals and other functions and the problem of this justice will become clear when examining the tools of justice.

Justice and the Means to Achieve It

Among the meanings of the word "means" in the Arabic language dictionaries are "everything through which a purpose is achieved," "tools that lead to the achievement of a specific end," "what is used to achieve a specific purpose"... etc.

The means and methods of achieving justice are divided into three categories: legal means, judicial means, and amicable means. Legal means divides into branches close in general characteristics and features, perhaps the most prominent of them are: legislation, custom, principles of religious laws, principles of natural law, and rules of fairness and justice and reconciliation...etc. As for friendly means, among the most prominent forms: mediation, conciliation, negotiations, reconciliation, good faith, and others.

However, the two most important means of achieving justice are: the law and the judiciary.

First: The Law

If you ask any law student, researcher, or practitioner, about "the law," he would immediately answer that it is a set of general, abstract rules that control the social behavior of an individual in his society, coupled with a worldly penalty imposed on those, who violate its prohibitions.

This answer describes the legal base but does not define law itself, i.e. law as a social phenomenon inherent in human society.

Law – as a social phenomenon – is the meeting and acquaintance of the wills of a group of human beings to defend their human existence, their material interests and their natural freedoms, even if it is necessary to use organized collective violence "legal penalty" to respond to the aggression against this group. This is the law in its pure sense.

In pure law, the legal base is formed over an indefinite period of time and through group members' practices of collective behaviors that reflect their reality, needs, and interests and from the repetition of those collective practices, the doctrine of compulsion is formed by the group and the prescribed penalty for violating the opposite or separate behavior to those practices became acceptable.

In pure law, each individual in the group participates in setting, enacting, and formulating the rules of this law and each individual pours his own interests at the bowl of those rules. In this law, everyone is equal before its discourse, costs, prohibitions, and advantages. It is the master of all and the servant of all, because the will of all is the reason for his existence.

So, the law is the work of the group, agreeing and getting acquainted with controlling its track in one direction or in a unified manner towards certain facts and events, without pressure on the group or directing or instructing from another group. This is "pure law" or law in its pure sense. Customary rules still represent this type of law until now, despite the decline in its role for the favor of official (state) law. The law in its pure space is the "unified force of the group" to respond to any attack on the interests of the group and to protect the equitable distribution of interests.

This law is the first qualified tool to be a tool for achieving justice in the realm of man.

In contrast to "pure law," "enacted law" stands. Perhaps the phrase "made up law" is more accurate in denoting the reality of this type of law. The "legal law" is the preformed law. In legal terminology, it means "legislation." Legislation has two types: original legislation that the competent legislative body "legislative authority" is qualified to enact and produce, the Subsidiary legislation set by the administration, "the executive authority," with a mandate from the legislative authority, according to specific controls. What is meant by law in this context is "original legislation."

The "enacted" law is also a collection of the wills of a limited group of individuals who agreed to produce a specific law that performs a specific function and although its rules are characterized by all the characteristics of the legal base, in terms of its generality, abstraction, and enjoyment of worldly punishment, but when analyzing and dismantling the elements of this law "the enacted/made up legislation," the problems of contradiction of these elements come to the surface.

The time required to produce this type of law does not usually exceed a few months and sometimes a few weeks. Rather, laws are produced within an hour of a day. This law, which was produced in hours, is intended to be applied for years to control behavior that was permissible and became prohibited overnight. Is it controlled by the justice of the law or by force of law?

This law is incapable of being a way to achieve justice, because the party that enacts it, whatever the name it bears (Parliament, the People's Assembly, the National Assembly...etc.) also suffers from several problems. In countries that claim that they are "democratic," the struggle between political parties to reach this legislative body is most intense. These parties use all kinds of hypocrisy and political bribery to reach their goal and the most powerful party is the one that controls the majority of the legislature and is the dominant and controlling party in law making and production.

The observer of the parliamentary elections of the most powerful Western Democracies easily notes that those, who occupy the majority of parliament seats and monopolize the power of legislation are the powerful political parties and blocs and that the minority is nothing more than being one of the requirements of Western democracy that is used when forming coalition governments and to be a "just another a number," whatever their slogans, ideologies, and programs.

When the scrutiny takes place over who brought these parties to the power of legislation, the people appear as the only actor who has the power to grant the parties the power to legislate in their name. But not all the people. There is a silent majority that did not participate in voting and a majority that does not meet the conditions for election and voting. Is it possible to say here that the law (enacted/made) represents the "conscience of the nation" or "the will of the people"? Even for those, who participated and took part in the election and voting, was their will free and sound while exercising their electoral right, or did some of them fall victim to electoral propaganda that is run by those, who are able to bear its exorbitant financial costs?

Therefore, the powerful are the ones who produce the law and control its direction and determine its goals and functions. How did these powerful people become powerful and occupied the power of legislation? Is it thanks to their broad popular base? Or thanks to the quality of their electoral programs? Or thanks to the strength of their charismatic personalities? They may have some of this and that, but the scandals emerging after the parliamentary elections in Western democracies show that access to parliament is usually thanks to financial and logistical support for transnational companies and major financial and economic conglomerates and even suspicious money (money laundering, prostitution, drugs, etc.) The influence of these companies and conglomerates has become clear on the law, especially the financial and economic laws, to the extent that the enacted law has become a protector of the interests of the powerful.

If this is the case of the enacted law "legislation" in "democratic" regimes, then the case in non-democratic regimes (individualism, totalitarianism, religious...etc), is extremely horrible. Appointing loyalists, buying the votes of simple people from the electorate and falsifying their wills under the authority's hearing and sight are all well-known ways to reach the legislative councils in the framework of mock elections. The result is that the powerful are the ones who make the law and produce it in accordance with their interests.

If the law, "legislation" in the democratic and non-democratic systems, is created and produced by the powerful, then what does this law protect?... The interests of the powerful, what function does it perform?... Protecting the powerful... What justice does it achieve?... the powerful justice.

Second: The Judiciary

The judiciary is seen as one of the tools for achieving justice. The judiciary has taken different forms and shapes throughout the ages. Human thought continues to invent new forms of Judiciary. From the judiciary of the family, the clan and the tribe, to the judiciary of temples, priests, and clerics, to the civil judiciary, from a voluntary agreement judiciary to an official "state judiciary" and from a conciliatory judiciary to a communal judiciary...etc.

The official judiciary (the state judiciary) is considered one of the most important and famous tools for achieving justice in our time and it is accepted and respected. But when analyzing this judiciary and dismantling its mechanisms of action, it turns out that it is not always the best way to achieve justice, given its authoritarian nature.

The official judiciary appeared mainly as an effect of the emergence of the authority of the political units, such as the authority of the clan, the authority of the tribe and the authority of the state, given that these units have a monopoly over the mechanism of oppression. It is then one of the tools of power in the political game, such as the army, political parties, parliament, and the media etc.

This authoritarian nature of the official judiciary appears in many forms and aspects. They appear in the laws organizing the judiciary, which gives the political authority the right to set the conditions for occupying the judicial position and it determines the litigant, the judge who hears his case, how and when to file it, and before which authority to file it. It also determines its fate, either by accepting it, rejecting it, not allowing it, or not hearing it etc. This judiciary is an authority of the state. The state is a political unit and all the components of this unit reflect the political feature of the state.

The official judiciary, "the state's judiciary," is based on the element of compulsion, which derives its strength and legitimacy from the fact that the judiciary itself is a state authority and a tool for controlling security and stability in it.

Compulsion is not limited to the mere consent of a person, who settles the dispute whose election or appointment was beyond the litigant decision, nor is he subject to litigation procedures in which the litigant had no role in enacting it. Rather, compulsion is represented in the acceptance of litigants of a judgment based on the conviction of a person other than the litigants themselves, without their will having a direct role in the formation or participation of the judge in this conviction. Compulsion also appears in submitting to specific mandatory appeal deadlines, in the absence of which the timing to appeal is expired and the appeal is based on specific reasons.

Compulsion also appears in the state's intervention to challenge a ruling that the litigants and the parties of the dispute have accepted, under the title "public order" or "public interest," as appeals of the Attorney General.

Compulsion also appears in the form of giving the court what is known in the language of the judiciary as "the discretionary power of the court" in understanding the reality in the case, in extracting its image and in assessing the evidence and its sufficiency. This power is beyond the oversight of even a court of law for the most part.

Compulsion also comes when the litigant is obliged to accept that the court is the supreme expert when the reports are weighted in a matter or a field that the judge did not take note of or did not read a text about.

The authoritarian nature of the official judiciary is reflected in the public prosecution system. This device declares itself to be a genuine opponent in the criminal case. It represents society – the state – in demanding the right of the state and society to punish and to implement the correct law. But it is an opponent who is never equal with the accused or even with the victim in procedural rights and duties. The public prosecution is part of the formation of the criminal court and its absence invalidates the ruling. As for the absence of the accused or the victim, the judgment is described as being present or as being present or absent. The Public Prosecution Office has the authority to take serious criminal measures in the criminal case, especially against the accused that affects his freedom and financial liability. It may imprison him in precaution, search him and his residence, prevent him from traveling, or seize his money. While the victim does not have the right to take any of these measures against the accused.

The Public Prosecution Authority has the authority to search and investigate evidence that supports its claim and to follow it wherever it is in decisions it issues, which is not owned by the rest of the criminal lawsuit opponents. As an indictment and investigation authority, it has the right to keep the criminal case before the accused for several reasons, including "lack of importance." What is the ethical basis for this type of keeping? Isn't the victim entitled to have his complaint heard by the judiciary? How is justice like? And what is its type in this case?

Among the problems of the official judiciary (the state judiciary) is that it is affected in terms of its type, forms, and multiple degrees, as well as in terms of its weakness and strength, its dependence and independence, by the political, social, economic and religious factors active within the community. In countries with true democratic regimes, the manifestations of democracy over the judiciary appear in the constitutional texts and laws of the judiciary that establish the foundations of a free and impartial judiciary, such as considering the judiciary a state authority, the independence of the judiciary, the inability of judges to be dismissed, the multiplicity of degrees of litigation and open ways of appealing its rulings and others. This is in contrast to countries in which totalitarian social systems are heading towards dictatorship, where the judiciary appears as one of the public facilities of the state and the judge becomes a public servant, the scope of his independence is narrowed, the ranks of the courts are reduced and non-judicial elements predominate in their formation.

The type of judiciary varies in countries with free economic systems and open markets, where specialized courts appear, especially in commercial and economic matters, such as commercial courts, real estate courts, securities courts, intellectual property and trademark courts etc. There are also many forms in these systems between the specialized official judiciary, the general judiciary, the consensual judiciary, and the conciliatory judiciary, which takes the form of mediation, good offices, conciliation, and reconciliation.

As for where the economic system is directed and guided, managed by the state bureaucracy and not by market mechanisms, the judiciary takes its form (its image) and performs its function in the light of the philosophy and requirements of the directed economy and the closed market, where the state relies in resolving economic disputes on administrative committees with jurisdiction or on the ideological and framed judiciary within the political thought of the ruling regime.

When religious ideas and metaphysical statements are dominant and direct social behavior, the judiciary is affected by these statements and ideas and what can be called "religious judiciary" or "religious courts" (church legitimacy, biblical, temple etc.). This is the judiciary that applies religious rules and places them in a higher rank than the constitution and makes the ruling issued by the religious courts a supreme divine pronouncement. The guardian is the holder of the general jurisdiction and the judiciary is an institution affiliated to him and the judges are his agents in issuing the final ruling in the dispute, it has the right to allocate the judiciary in time and place and it has the right to transcend the rules and procedures of litigation and issue judgments and he has the authority to have the final say in the dispute etc.

On the contrary, in secular societies, it is the law established by the human legislator through the competent legislative bodies and institutions, which determines the forms, shapes and types of the judiciary, which means that the judiciary, whatever its type, shape or form, is a true and honest expression about the will of the nation and the prevailing trends in society.

The best thing to say is that judiciary of this nature and of this problem, cannot rise with its own justice, so how can it rise with the justice of others. What this judiciary produces is the justice of the judiciary, not the judiciary of justice.

Justice... Its Protection

It was previously emphasized that justice in realm of man is a supreme human value that is necessary for the integrity of man's life. But this value may be eroded by the voluntary and conscious actions of the man himself. This erosion appears in several forms, such as: loss of respect for the law, misdistribution of wealth and benefits among members of society, the emergence of a gap between social classes, corruption of the judiciary and those in charge of implementing the law, tyranny of the ruling system...in addition to other forms.

The corrosion of justice, means the deterioration of its basic properties as a result of the interaction of corrosive forms with the corrosive medium. Among the characteristics of justice are: goodness, mercy, equality, benevolence, fairness, and virtue. To clarify the process of corrosion of justice, we give the example of the following "equation": Corrupt judiciary "the form of erosion" + absence of the law or its lack of clarity "medium of erosion" + interaction = disappearance of justice "one of the properties of justice."

Whatever the idea of justice, i.e. the mental image of it, or the definition by which it is defined, its corrosion in any way, reflects negatively on the society and its security, stability, well-being, and sustainability as a good and qualified society to be a habitat for the human being whose life is unstable in the absence of justice.

Protecting justice from corrosion is a collective responsibility shared by the state with its official authorities and institutions, because justice is the basis of the ruling and society with its civil institutions. The same applies to the individual with his human and moral motives, because justice is a human necessity essential for the integrity of man's life and the preservation of his rights and interests from being exposed to dangers or threats.

The protection of justice from corrosion passes through the following defenses:

Conscience

It is well established that conscience contributes to the advancement and progress of mankind, by guiding and directing the person towards truth and away from falsehood, adhering to justice and staying away from injustice, adhering to goodness and staying away from evil and adhering to virtue and staying away from vice...etc. With conscience, a person is able to distinguish whether an action is right or wrong, just or unjust. By it, a person feels regretful when the actions he commits conflict with his moral values while he feels righteousness when his actions are consistent with moral values. The conscience represents a hidden call rooted in the human soul, which commands its owner to be fair in speech and action.

Conscience is the subject of a number of social and human sciences, such as philosophy, psychology, ethics and religions and every science deal with the subject through its curriculum and approaches.

In the field of philosophy, conscience is a complex of emotional experiences based on a person's understanding of the moral responsibility for his behavior in society. The degree to which a person submits to the call of his conscience is affected by the circumstances that surround him, the environment in which he lives and the values and ideals in which he was brought up and believed in. This is because conscience is not inherited, but acquired by a person. A person can increase his conscience over the actions he performs by reflecting on the importance of good human values, as this serves as a driving force for self-discipline.

The conscience is that hidden voice that commands a person to direct his will towards choosing a matter among other things in which he has the ability to choose. The role of conscience in protecting justice from erosion appears through its effect on directing a person towards every action that is consistent with the values of justice, such as judging with equity, staying away from injustice and speaking the truth and rejecting everything that contradicts those values even if the violating action is consistent with his instincts and desires. Participation in rigging elections, profiting from a job and giving false testimony in front of the judiciary to get rid of an opponent or rival, are all actions that may bring pleasure, happiness or benefit to the doer, but they form an instinctive, lustful, possessive benefit that moves away from the "supreme ego" and even from the "average ego."

Virtuous Ethics

Virtuous ethics are the set of principles and values that people in a society agree on their highness and sophistication and the need to follow them behaving towards themselves and their society and towards other individuals and societies. The origin of these ethics is the human instinct, which is created to be good. It is therefore "natural ethics" as opposed to "philosophical ethics" and "religious ethics."

What is meant by "natural ethics" is the set of moral feelings, virtues, and ideals that are formed in man on the basis of his natural cognitive means according to the circumstances of his life. It stems from the duties that his life requires and imposes on him, without the person returning to a rational analysis, nor to deep philosophical thinking, nor to ideas and lofty ideals that transcend the reality of life as he lives it and as he acts within its limits.

Every civilization, nation and people have their own virtuous ethics that guide them to creativity, innovation, and the dissemination of love and peace and reflect the spirit of that civilization, nation, and people such as "Islamic Ethics," "Arab Ethics," "Indian Ethics," "Chinese Ethics," "European Ethics" etc.

"Arab ethics" is famous for its moral values and principles that have become proverbial. It is sufficient to look at the literature of pre-Islamic poets to know the extent to which the virtuous ethics of the Arabs are rooted. Here, the Arab poet "Damra bin Damra al-Nahshly" expresses his duty towards his people and his feeling of solidarity with them, saying:

And I am not trying to protect myself,
but I am defending the neighborhood.

And the circle of virtuous ethics extends in its subject to many and varied principles and values, for example but not limited to, the principle of "fulfillment of the covenant," the principle of "support your brother whether he is an oppressor or the oppressed," the principle of "pardon when able" and the principle of "goodness" neighborhood. And the values of chastity, honest testimony, forgiveness, justice, mercy, altruism, generosity, courage etc.

As for the extent of morals, it extends to begin with a person's relationship with himself, his family, his clan, his community, and other individuals and groups and even to the relations of states to each other.

The role of virtuous ethics in protecting justice from corrosion emerges from the fact that these ethics elevate the human soul to the point of transcendence. Every action or statement that leads to good is justice.

Judiciary

There is an eternal relationship between justice and the judiciary, they are inseparable. The judiciary is the house of justice and justice is the home of the judiciary. Philosophers have talked about the judiciary as one of the most prominent means of protecting justice, such as Plato and Aristotle. Moreover, the Arab philosopher Ibn-e-Sina tackled the same concept in his book "The Just City." The philosophers of the Age of Enlightenment linked justice and the judiciary in many ways.

But what is judiciary that can protect justice from corrosion?

The inability of the state judiciary, the "official judiciary" to achieve justice, has been explained by its official nature, which is steeped in authoritarianism. It is by its nature that it only offers authoritarian justice (the justice of power).

The judiciary that is able to protect justice from erosion, the "non-authoritarian judiciary," has specific features, the first of which is that it is the judiciary in which the will of the state "authority" is at its lowest level, in terms of establishing this judiciary, managing it, running it, or in terms of litigation procedures before it. Issuing and appealing judgments.

Whereas, the will of the disputants appears clearly and predominantly in most of the affairs of this judiciary.

This type of "non-authoritarian" judiciary takes different arbitrary frameworks, most notably arbitration, conciliation, mediation, good faith and societal judiciary, which is a court framework that allows a wide scope for the wills of the disputants to resolve their disputes while giving a complementary role to the will of the state, "the official judiciary."

The second characteristic of a judiciary qualified to protect justice is that it opens the door to appeal against its rulings before a higher judiciary, according to procedures and dates that the litigants agree to follow and comply with i.e. not to be imposed on them. Here, we face a serious question "How can justice be protected, if the authority has the right to appeal a ruling that the litigants have accepted under the pretext of the interest of the law, the public interest, or other pretexts of the authority, such as the appeals of the Public Prosecution Office?"

The third characteristic of such type of judiciary is the emergence of the active participation of the litigants in creating the judicial ruling that settles their dispute. The more this participation emerges, the closer the judgment is to the judicial truth. It is a fact that declares that justice has been restored.

The non-authoritarian judiciary is the one qualified to protect justice from corrosion and it is a judiciary that has roots in our Arab and Islamic history. For the pre-Islamic Arabs, this type of judiciary was prevalent and it was accepted and respected by the litigants to the extent that the arbitrator's ruling was finding its way to implementation without problems or troubles, in the absence of the institution of the "execution judge"... Why?... Because the ruling is the result of the will and agreement of the two parties of the conflict, it is ruled by an arbitrator free from the constraints of authority, even if it is the authority of a tribe's chief.

The Law

Just as the judiciary has a close relationship with justice, the law has the same relationship with it; as one of the functions of the law is to achieve justice. However, the enacted law "legislation" suffers from many problems that prevent it from being a means of protecting justice, the least of which is its problematic issues or its oligarchy.

The oligarchic nature of enacted law calls upon the advocate of justice to search for other types of law that bear the characteristics of law qualified to protect justice from corrosion; patterns that make room for the will of the person addressed by the legal rule to participate in its enactment, creation or choice. In this space, customary law, conventional law and voluntary law emerge as "voluntary laws."

Customary Law

The structure of this law is based on the "community will" of the community as a whole; in its members, its customs, its traditions, its religious, social and cultural heritage, its social and religious function, and its interrelationships with its peers. This will, which represents the community and expresses its spirit and conscience, corresponds to and identifies with duties to be performed and obligations to be completed. That is, it is a human behavior emanating from the group that takes place on a regular, steady and permanent basis and is respected by everyone to the extent of a firm belief in its obligation and enjoys the worldly reward.

Customary law arises away from the influence and control of groups with material interests or political ambitions, or ideas and ideologies seeking to gain power.

It is a law that arises from the repetition of behaviors that the group has accepted after it has experienced its benefit and goodness in order to protect its interests. It is a law that represents time as an important element in its emergence, development and stability; as it is not the result of an emergency event or a casual political trend.

Consensual Law

This law arises from a "contract" agreement concluded between its parties to resolve their disputes and differences arising from their personal ties, or to distribute benefits and interests among them, according to rules and procedures agreed upon among them. It is therefore a law that is enacted, promulgated, published and terminated, by the wills of those addressed with its provisions, who are themselves the legislators and hence emerges the will of this law.

Among the manifestations of this will is freedom from the constraints of the authority, from the outbidding of political parties and parliamentary blocs when enacting legislation and from the complexities of the procedures that dominate the process of producing the enacted law. It is pure voluntary law.

Because it is a "consensual law," it is a means not only to achieve justice, but even to protect it from corrosion by virtue of its voluntary nature. The will of the addressees by this consensual law determines the amount of pleasure or pain that each addressee receives, that is, the amount of benefit or harm that will be in the hands of each addressee and when the determination of pleasure and pain is agreed upon, justice still retains its characteristics.

Due to its voluntary nature, the availability of moral freedom among the addressees of the consensual law is a condition for its validity and enforcement. Satisfaction with this law must be true. The validity of consent requires that the will of the persons addressed by the law be sound and free from defects such as error, coercion, fraud, and exploitation. It also requires that they will be conscious, mature, and issued by a fully qualified person.

The consensual law is highlighted in the field of arbitration contracts and the conditions or stipulations attached to them, as well as conciliation contracts and dispute settlement contracts in the field of investment and private companies. This law also stands out clearly in the field of international law, as the majority of its rules are conventions that take the form of international treaties and agreements.

Optional Law

The optional law is another type of the "voluntary law" pattern, in which the will emerges through the space of freedom that the individual possesses in choosing the law to abide by. The individual chooses with his free will – while being conscious and aware of the facts of things and matters – the law that he thinks – as entailed by his own interests – he should be addressed by. This law may be customary, conventional or state-related "official."

This pattern is achieved by the law, even if the choice is based on the mere implementation of one text or specified texts of a law, or even through enacting a guiding law. When the law gives the plaintiff the option to renew his case or dismissing it and he chooses the dismissal, he chooses what he deems in his best interest. Such example reflects many cases, such as appealing or not challenging the ruling, accepting or rejecting conciliation, relinquishing the complaint or proceeding with it.... In these and similar examples, the individual is not faced with an inevitable imposition, but rather a choice to pick the law.

When contractually obligated parties prefer to apply a law other than the law of the state in which the contract is made to their obligations and when a non-citizen chooses to apply the provisions of the Personal Status Law "the law of the state of residence" to the "law of the state of nationality," he has voluntarily chosen the law in which he sees his interest will be fulfilled.

There are laws prepared by international or regional organizations on various topics called "model laws" or "guideline laws," the aim of which is to help countries reform and update their laws, such as the model laws prepared by the United Nations Commission on International Trade Law "INCITRAL" and the guiding laws set by the League of Arab States. Although it does not in itself have any legal force, nothing prevents it from agreeing to implement its texts in disputes that can be resolved by conciliation, arbitration, or consent.

In such examples and the likes, the will of the person being addressed by the law appears as a fundamental basis in choosing the law that corresponds to his interests.

In short, with regard to talking about the judiciary as a protector of justice from wearing away, the voluntary law is the guarantor thereof to fulfill such role.

Justice Is the End

Justice among a man's world is a supreme human value, but it is not an absolute value, as is justice in its supreme being. It is in the value of humanity that its existence is linked to the end of the human being, like the rest of the higher human values, such as good and evil, selfishness and giving, beauty and ugliness, generosity, and stinginess...etc. It is all about man in his conscious and aware human behavior of the realities and natures of things.

It is from the nature of the highest human values that they occupy a place in the moral aspect of man, that is, in his spirit, soul, and morals. This aspect is the essence of man as a rational, speaking, free creature that possesses moral freedom. However, animals do share some of these values with humans such as mercy, sadness and selflessness, except it does so instinctively, not as a moral value. Unless the highest human values are practiced through the person himself with his feelings and emotions, then – the highest human value – is neither valuable nor human.

Justice is a supreme human value and it is one of the prerequisites of human civilization and it has both material and moral aspects. The material aspect is formed from by words, actions, and attitudes of the human being as well as the circumstances surrounding it, whether such are of social, economic, environmental, climatic, or geographical nature.

As for the moral aspect of justice, it is represented in the feelings, sentiments, emotions, and desires of the people of justice, that is, the people who participate in the production of justice as a human value, with their personal traits that revolve between good and evil, honesty and lies, intelligence and naivety; or social attributes such as wealth and poverty, knowledge and ignorance, elevation and lowliness etc.

Justice is not the product of one person, but the product of the concerted efforts of all the persons of justice. The judge is not the only person, who makes justice through his judicial rulings; however, this is shared by the "Plaintiff," the "Defendant," the "Witnesses," the "Experts," the "Lawyers" and the "Members of the Public Prosecution." Each of these contributes to the production of justice, but the contribution of each one of them is colored by the color of his feelings and cultural, religious, and social background. When the judge listens to the arguments of the litigating parties, the testimonies of witnesses and the reports of experts, he is sometimes filled with a range of varied feelings of happiness, sadness, anger, and regret. Sometimes he feels helpless and sometimes victorious. Through all these contradictory feelings and emotional states, he comes out with the wisdom of his "judgment," which is the title of truth. When the victim, the "harmed party," narrates his statements about the incident, brings before the judge the events of the incident, recounting them with his feelings, emotional state, pain, and sentiments. The same applies to the rest of the persons of justice making the judge form his belief in the case by taking from the statements of these persons and then ruling in the case.

Despite the high position that justice occupies amongst human beings and despite its importance to the integrity of his life and despite the literature that he formulated in glorifying justice and exalting it, it leads justice consciously and deliberately to its end.

The end of justice is by stripping the same of its human value and this abstraction appears clearly in the means of achieving justice; especially the "law" and the judiciary. When the law turns into an arithmetic operation or a mathematical equation that produces a number that was unknown, then it is stripped of its human value. It is also when the person responsible for its implementation does not have any role in imparting aspects of his humanity to the implementation process.

It is stripped of its human value when the person being addressed by law is seen as just one of his own persons who has committed one of his prohibitions and he must be reprimanded with the penalty assigned to him, whether it is a criminal, civil, procedural, or disciplinary penalty. A foreign juvenile, who commits a transgressive crime is deported from the country after the ruling becomes final, without any consideration of the humanitarian aspects of this juvenile or his family.

Justice is stripped of its human value, when the judge has no choice but to prescribe punishment for the availability of presumptions of the (legal) rule without having the legal authority to highlight his human feelings in assessing the circumstances that necessitate mitigating or aggravating the penalty.

Justice is stripped of its human value when the judiciary is entrusted to incompetent persons and when it loses its independence and impartiality.

But the end of justice is tragic when it leaves the bosom of man and into the bosom of the machine. There are those, who call for the use of robots (robots, cyborgs bodies) that are equipped with artificial intelligence simulating natural human intelligence, as a means of achieving justice, specifically when playing the role of judges, arbitrator, or mediator. Meaning that it is entrusted with the task of adjudicating disputes, cases and lawsuits and issuing judgments and decisions that are binding and decisive.

The advocates are based on a set of facts that reveal the success of the "analytic" robot in accomplishing and completing complex tasks in a way that exceeds the skill, accuracy and speed of what a natural person does, such as performing precise surgical operations and laboratory tests of dozens of samples within minutes and providing the precise results. It is also used in directing planes, ships, trains, and other means of transportation, with high efficiency and with minimal risks and errors.

They argue that this machine has the ability to provide social advice to those, who are about to choose their life partner and advice to those, who suffer from psychological or social problems. These advocates conclude that this robot can issue decisions in legal and human rights cases, if it is fed with legal and judicial data.

When the machine is a means to achieve justice, man has lost the humanity of justice. Hence, man faces the justice of the machine instead of the justice machine.

The State and Justice

The state; the most renowned and most powerful moral figure. The secret of its fame and power is driven from the fact that it is the only body among the societies of law that has a monopoly over the mechanism of power, "legal violence" and sovereignty together. With such the state imposes its will and hegemony on the basic elements of its components "the people – the region – the government." Whatever the political system of the state is, it remains a repressive apparatus that has been legalized in order to serve the interests of those, who hold power and sovereignty.

The idea of "public interest," "public order," and "public security" is an oppressive trilogy created by the state itself to maintain dominance and sovereignty over the elements of its basic components as a sovereign figure. It determines the elements and components of this trilogy, laying out its standards and controls and setting the means to achieve and protect them.

The army, the police, the security sector, the judiciary, the law, the parties, and the media remain among the means that the state uses to reinforce its repressive nature. Moreover, all of them – the means – work according to its directions, whatever their system and political thought. Those trends are set and formulated by the executive and legislative ruling elite. The (state-official) justice comes in the form of "legal justice" and "judicial justice," as one of those means.

State (official) justice is subject to the will of the state and the scope of its functional space is limited to the triad of "public interest," "public order" and "public security." It is obligated to adjust everything the state says that it is a public interest, everything it considers to be public order and all the security measures it takes as "justice." Removing a neighborhood inhabited by poor and low-income people, to build a road, is a "just act" even if thousands of neighborhood residents remain homeless for years. Practicing gambling on the side of the road is considered an act that violates public order, while it is considered "legal" to practice the same action inside gambling halls, even if the spatial separation between the two places (the road and the hall) is a few meters. The gathering of a number of workers to demand their rights is considered a breach of public security, while the gathering of thousands of people in the same place to watch an entertainment party is considered a "legal" act.

These examples and the likes, highlight the will of the state as if it were "justice."

State justice is the product of an enacted law and an official judiciary and this outcome bears the characteristic of "directed justice." It is justice that serves the state's orientations in its political, social, economic, and cultural paths and choices, which may not necessarily be in the interest of the people or the individual.

The nature of the state as a sovereign juridical person does not allow the rule of "value justice," which takes precedence over justice as a supreme human value, over "functional justice," which is a tool for consolidating the state's repression when it performs its functions.

Justice... The Requirements of the Movement of Life

If justice in a man's world is contaminated with the sins of its inhabitants and colored by the interests and the ideas of its sects, then it is difficult to find justice that can meet the demands of the fast-paced daily life movement, its multi-interests and parties across borders and continents.

In the light of the multiplicity, diversity and intertwining of the movement of life, its quantity and quality as well as its vertical and horizontal extension and in scope inside and outside, the requirements of protecting this movement necessitate the need to create a form of justice that controls it in a way that provides a fair distribution of benefits amongst the conflicting and intersecting interests of people active in the movement of daily life within the society in which we live.

The movement of life within a society is driven by the interests of its members, groups, political and civil organizations as well as by the interests of men of power, leaders of political parties, leaders of the army and police, media men and the judiciary. Such interests often clash and conflict, creating a state of anxiety and turmoil, unless the state intervenes to control it through its various soft and coarse means, among which is the creation of justice that performs the function of "controlling the pace of the demands of life," that is, creating "controlling justice."

The controlling justice is the prevailing feature of daily life and by which the state dominates its residents, who in turn deal with it in order to preserve their interests resulting from their role in the movement of daily life in society, as any objection to this justice deprives them of reaping the benefits of the movement of life. This objection may also lead to considering them as enemies of the state.

In many of its characteristics and features, "regulatory justice" identifies with official "state" justice. It is – the controlling justice – "functional justice" whose function is to control the movement of daily life within society and it has nothing to do with justice as a supreme human value. It is the "framed justice" that operates within specific frameworks and regulations that the state sets and controls. It is also the "compulsory justice," as the state with its authority and sovereignty obliges people to accept it; and it is the state that sets and defines the means of achieving such justice. It is "codified justice."

This is the justice of our lives as humans!

End of Text.
May God be Our Guide…

The Author
Ajman in the evening of Friday 25/1/2018 AD